PIONEER DIESELS
AROUND LONDON

Pat Avery

Noodle *N.B.* Books

ISBN 978-1-906419-82-0

First published in 2012 by Kevin Robertson under the **NOODLE BOOKS** imprint
PO Box 279, Corhampton, SOUTHAMPTON. SO32 3ZX

www.noodlebooks.co.uk

Printed in England by Berforts Information Press.

Front cover - Western diesel-hydraulic 2,700hp Type 4 class leader No. D1000 'Western Enterprise' eases off the turntable at Old Oak Common on 9 January 1966 under the watchful eye of depot maintenance staff.

Photo: the late Andrew Smith / authors collection

Frontispiece - Extensively trialled over the proposed routes of operation prior to introduction was the prototype of the highly successful High Speed Train concept, unit No.252.001, seen here at St.Pancras whilst on a demonstration run over the Midland main line.

Pat Avery collection

Rear cover - Parcels traffic was always big business on the Western Region in the London area. The 1959 built Gloucester Railway Carriage & Wagon Co. motor parcels vans perpetuated the idea of using dedicated service vehicles for these services, started by their predecessors, Nos. W17W & W34W, of GWR origin. One of the GRCW Co. units 'purrs' on to the Greenford loop at Drayton Green Halt. *The On Line Video collection*

INTRODUCTION

When Sir Brian Robertson, Chairman of the British Transport Commission, announced plans for the modernisation of British Railways in January 1955 the system was already at crisis point, frequently facing a huge budget deficit. The new plan advocated the replacement of steam with diesel and electric motive power, but there was, in comparison to the large steam fleet, a mere handful of main line diesels, railcars and assorted shunters then in operation.

Before large scale dieselisation of the network started, the BTC commissioned designs for small batch production from various manufacturers in order to evaluate those most suitable. These were classified in power ranges as; Type A: up to 1,000hp, Type B: 1,000 - 1,500hp and Type C: 2,000hp and above. Two years later in 1957, a further addition was included to fill the gap between Types B and C.

With the sole exception of English Electric, who had previous association with both the London Midland & Scottish, and Southern railways, the achilles' heel was the lack of experience in diesel locomotive construction on this scale, particularly by those who subsequently became involved in the process.

Under increasing political pressure to hasten the transition from steam, large orders for new diesel locomotives were placed with British manufacturers. In this seemingly free for all, the Western Region went off at a tangent by opting for diesel-hydraulic machines based on German technology, well before any idea of performance or reliability could be properly considered.

Visually too the result was that design consultants, such as Wilkes & Ashmore, frequently found themselves faced with a 'clean-up' operation due to lack of co-operation and a marked reluctance to take outside guidance.

Gradually realisation dawned that there needed to be some co-ordination in the policy of industrial design, which led to the creation of a design panel in 1956 to advise on the best way to achieve greater standards of appearance and unity.

In 1957 the power ranges were redefined by the British Transport Commission using numerical digits in place of the previous letters:

Type 1	750 – 1,000hp
Type 2	1,000 – 1,250hp
Type 3	1,500 – 1,750hp
Type 4	2,000 – 2,500hp
Type 5	3,000hp and above

The subsequent failure of the Modernization Plan to deliver all as promised led to a major distrust of BR's financial planning abilities by the Treasury, and even worse an unmitigated disaster for the British taxpayer, who ultimately ended up footing the bill.

In the aftermath of the Beeching Report of the early 1960's, the contents of which attempted to redress the balance of grossly over-estimated operational requirements and spiralling costs, the National Traction Plan published in 1967, envisaged rationalising locomotive types from 28 down to 15. This dealt a knock-out blow to the diesel hydraulics, as well as the less successful classes deemed to be non-standard, thus by 1975, with the exception of the Western class of diesel-hydraulics, this vision had been accomplished.

To those who were there; the enthusiast, and even the casual observer, the pioneer days represented a fascinating era when the operating regions, largely based on pre-nationalised management structures, retained a high degree of autonomy and control.

Most railway photographers reserved their expensive colour film for steam, and as a result quality images of diesels are relatively thin on the ground. It is said a picture paints a thousand words and in that sense I am fortunate to have inherited my late cousin's Andrew Smith's slide collection, which along with other contributors' work has allowed me to re-kindle past memories before the point is reached where personal and anecdotal recollections are lost forever.

Along with many other railway minded people met along the way, I was privileged enough to have witnessed the best era for diesel traction in London.

Thank you for the camaraderie.

Pat Avery
Exeter Devon, 2012

WESTERN REGION

On Thursday 24 August 1961 Warship diesel-hydraulic 2,200hp Type 4 No.D822 'Hercules' prepares to leave Paddington with the 1.30pm "The Royal Duchy" to Penzance. With ever increasing numbers of 'Warships' rolling off the production line, the WR management wasted no time displacing the ex-GWR 'King' and 'Castle' class steam locomotives from the principal West of England express services. However this tenure was brief as by 1964 the more powerful 'Western' diesel-hydraulics became the ruling incumbents of these duties. In 1968 aspirations for accelerated timings between Paddington and Plymouth brought a revival in fortunes for the class. The 'Westerns', unable to cope with the heavy load requirements, allowed the 'Warships' to operate the flagship services once more, this time hunting in pairs. To facilitate this, multiple-working equipment was re-instated on Nos.D819/22-4/27-29/31/32 and 866-69. Despite increases in traffic levels this strategy was not without problems, as failure of one locomotive meant the other could not maintain timings. By 1970 the timetable had been recast into separate Torbay and Plymouth trains so reverting to single locomotive haulage. *Pat Avery*

Saturday 12 July 1974 sees Western diesel-hydraulic 2,700hp Type 4 No. D1026 'Western Centurion', in the final livery of rail blue with full yellow ends, head past Westbourne Park en-route from a clean at the Kensal Green washing apron to head 1B43, the 18.30 Paddington-Plymouth. This was the return leg of an out and home diagram which had seen the Laira based diesel working up earlier in the day on the 05.10 Penzance-Paddington, the Western having taken over at Plymouth. After overhauls and heavy maintenance of the Westerns ceased at Swindon, Laira became the adopted home of the 'thousands' until the final class members were withdrawn in 1977. *Pat Avery*

Framed by period Collett and Hawksworth coaching stock, Beyer-Peacock diesel-hydraulic 1,700hp 'Hymek' Type 3 No. D7003 runs light engine into Paddington; the sleek contours of the Wilkes & Ashmore design readily apparent. Such was the haste to accelerate the pace of dieselisation that forty-five locomotives of this class were ordered without the construction of a single prototype. The manufacturer had hoped for a build number far higher than the eventual 101 total that was sanctioned by the British Rail Board at Marylebone. Considered opinion has it that this decision, coupled with other economic factors, undoubtedly contributed towards Beyer-Peacock's demise. The MD870 16-cylinder Maybach engine was the largest used in the hydraulics, generally giving good performance across the power range. Despite peculiarities with the Mekydro transmission, notably throttling down as a gear change was made; they were highly revered by railwaymen.

Amyas Crump collection

In early 1962 the Beyer Peacock 'Hymek' Type 3 diesels replaced steam on the principal Paddington-South Wales expresses, often putting in highly commendable performances for motive power 'punching above their weight'. Inevitably the intensive diagrams worked resulted in failures which required substitution. One such rescue in the autumn of that year saw the unusual appearance of Western diesel-hydraulic 2,700hp Type 4 No.D1005 'Western Venturer', in original BR Maroon livery with lemon yellow buffer beams, piloting an unidentified 'Hymek' into Paddington.

.Amyas Crump collection

Left - The merits of hydraulic versus electric transmission had already been debated and the future decided when vanquished and victor stood side by side at Old Oak Common depot on 8 January 1967 - respectively Western diesel-hydraulic 2,700hp Type 4 No.1019 'Western Challenger', and Brush diesel-electric 2,750hp Type 4 No.D1604. Six years later in May 1973, 'Western Challenger' earned the distinction of becoming the first Western withdrawal: No. D1604, re-numbered under TOPS as 47.476, lasted a further 20 years until cut up by C J Booth, Rotherham in 2004.

The late Andrew Smith / authors collection.

Above - Green reigns supreme! An impressive diesel-hydraulic line up around the turntable at Old Oak Common on 15 January 1966 sees North British 1,100hp Type 2, and Beyer Peacock (Hymek) 1,700hp Type 3 locomotives, before the repaint into corporate rail blue livery had started. The front end detail design variation of the NBL Type 2s is clearly visible, featuring the unusual sideways folding head-code discs fitted to No.D6327, as opposed to the split head code box arrangement fitted to other class members portrayed by No.D6350. Nearest the camera 'Hymek' Type 3 No.D7067 has suffered cab side collision damage somewhat detracting from the otherwise smart design. *The late Andrew Smith / authors collection.*

Early operating experiences proved that the Warship diesels were underpowered for top-link services. In response Swindon gained approval to design and build a new locomotive to the BTC Type 4 specification with two Maybach MD655 diesel engines linked to a 3-speed Voith hydraulic transmission intended to achieve the required power output. One drawback of this arrangement and which blighted the Westerns' performance, was the design mismatch between the engines and transmission: meaning that the top gear ratio was too high for the torque characteristics of the engine. This resulted in work-weary locomotives, or those due for overhaul, underperforming. To be fair the BTC virtually gave the Western a free hand in the external design, resulting in one of the finest creations ever seen on the rail network. On 15 January 1966 No.D1071 'Western Renown' sporting the well suited maroon livery carried by all but three members of the class during the mid-60s, roars into life outside Old Oak Common factory.

The late Andrew Smith /authors collection

D6352

Insert - A close up study of North British Loco Company builders' works plate as originally fitted to NBL 1,100hp Type 2 No.D6352. When members of the class were repainted into corporate rail blue from mid 1967 onwards, the builders' plates were removed from their position under the numbers. Two were discarded, whilst the remaining plates were fitted to the centre body side valance, one on each side. Since it was common for these valances to fall off, very few of the plates have survived. *The late Andrew Smith / authors collection.*

Squeezed in alongside staff cars parked at Old Oak Common depot on 8 January 1967 is work stained North British 1,100hp Type 2 No. D6348. Of note is the steam age shed code plate fixed to the side valance: '81A' indicating the home depot. From the day they were ordered by the British Transport Commission this class was the locomotive the Western Region did not want. The expectation was for lightweight diesel-hydraulic engines of German design. What they got was a design specification identical to the 1,000hp diesel-electric D6100s also constructed by NBL, in that used riveted and welded section beams and cross-members, topped by a heavy gauge steel floor with aluminium bodywork. In short they were built like tanks. The BTC rationale was that comparisons could then be made between similar machines one with hydraulic and the other having electric transmission. Unfortunately, and like their diesel-electric cousins, they were troublesome when new but to the credit of WR maintenance staff these issues were gradually resolved and they eventually settled down to give reliable service. The collapse of NBL in 1962 did little to alleviate problems later in the decade when increasing numbers of engine and transmission components needed replacing. Until replacement diesel-electric Brush and BR/Sulzer Type 2s became available the only option, rather expensively, was to use withdrawn locomotives as donors in order to keep other members of the class operational.

The late Andrew Smith / authors collection

(An attempt was made to preserve class member No. D6319 and purchase terms were agreed with BR. Unfortunately before the purchaser could take delivery, D6319 was accidentally cut up by staff at Swindon Works. In recompense BR offered the purchaser a Warship class locomotive at the same price and No. D821 '*Greyhound*' thus became the first preserved ex-BR mainline diesel locomotive.)

Old Oak Common was the last of the Western Region's principal diesel facilities to become operational. The conversion from being a steam shed began in 1964 and was completed in October 1965. The substantial steam era roundhouse complex dating from 1906 was demolished and a new diesel shed was built on the site of the former southern turntable. Although now uncovered, the western turntable and associated stalls was retained. In addition, heavy maintenance continued in the former GWR repair shop, commonly referred to as the 'factory', outside of which on a Sunday afternoon in January 1967 engines awaiting duty / attention included: (from left) Brush diesel-electric 2,750hp Type 4 No.D1746, North British diesel-hydraulic 1,100hp Type 2 No.D6347, snowplough-fitted Hymek diesel-hydraulic 1,700hp Type 3 No.D7026, a trio of unidentified diesel-electric 350hp 0-6-0 shunters, and another Hymek diesel-hydraulic. The concrete fence, just visible in the right background, separated the depot environs from the towpath of the adjacent Grand Union Canal. Over time damaged and broken panels allowed fairly easy access to the site without the prospect of immediate detection! *Photo: the late Andrew Smith / authors collection*

Doyen of the Western class 2,700hp diesel-hydraulics, No.D1000 '*Western Enterprise*' emerged from Swindon works in late 1961 in an experimental all-over desert sand livery with red buffer beams. However problems with the safety of permanent way staff working at trackside not seeing or hearing approaching diesels, led to Warship hydraulic No.D845 '*Sprightly*' being trialled with yellow warning panels surrounding the route indicator boxes in an attempt to improve visibility. This modification was then adopted by BR and applied to all locomotives; '*Western Enterprise*' received this treatment in November 1962, and is seen wearing this colour scheme outside the factory at Old Oak Common on 9 April 1964. A repaint to maroon livery would follow later in the year, and again to rail blue with full yellow ends in June 1967. *Modern Image Slides*

Following the introduction of a locomotive hauled Manchester Pullman service over the newly electrified lines between Euston and Manchester, the two six-car Midland Pullman diesel units formerly operating on the London Midland Region were rendered superfluous from April 1966 and transferred to the Western Region to augment the three eight car units already in use there. With five Pullman formations now available on the WR there was much debate as to how best to utilize the trains. One option, from 6 March 1967, was a mid-day Oxford Pullman service introduced with one of the six-car sets, this also had a proportion of the former all first class seating converted to second class. Intended as a middle of the day working for one of the sets employed on the morning and evening Bristol Pullman turns, this speculative but unsuccessful venture was primarily aimed at tourists, but failed to attract sufficient numbers and was short lived. The other six-car set went down to Bristol and back as an off-peak Bristol Pullman, both units coming up to Paddington in the morning, and returning together in the early evening. Prior to the introduction of this change, Motor Brake First M60090, still in Midland Pullman branding, receives attention in the Pullman maintenance shed at Old Oak Common on 8 January 1967. *The late Andrew Smith / authors collection*

As the fifties drew to a close, the British Transport Commission realising the importance of pleasing looks, gave the design consultants a virtual free hand in styling modernisation era new builds. What transpired with the 'Western' class diesel-hydraulics, introduced progressively from late 1961 onwards, was a very elegant locomotive indeed, designed jointly by Misha Black, professor of industrial design at the Royal College of Art in London, and William Beresford-Evans of the Design Research Unit. Forming a stark contrast with the bland, it might even be said 'ugly' front end of the North British D63xx behind, 2,700hp Type 4 No.D1024 'Western Huntsman', is seen at Old Oak Common on 9 January 1966 sporting the much admired maroon livery with small yellow warning panels. Seven members of the class were painted green when new, of which only three, Nos.D1004/D1036 and D1037 went straight from this to rail blue. *The late Andrew Smith / authors collection*

Once the M4 and M40 motorways became operational, concerns grew over threats to the valuable upmarket commuter traffic between Oxford, Reading and London. To help preserve market share, the Western drafted in Swindon Inter City DMUs displaced from Portsmouth-Cardiff services. Constructed to a superior finish, they had more in common with BR MK1 coaching stock, having 64' 6" underframes and commonwealth B4 bogies, which gave a very comfortable ride quality. Ten four car sets had been built, five of which had buffet provision. Gangways at the outer ends allowed a set of each to be used, giving access throughout. In 1970 the buffet cars were withdrawn so reducing half the sets to three car units. In May 1973 set L715, minus buffet, leads a similar but four-car unit through the suburbs at West Ealing on a Paddington to Oxford semi-fast. *Pat Avery*

Opposite top - . Taking a circuitous route through the West London suburbs at South Greenford in order to regain the GW main line at Hanwell is North British Locomotive Co. Warship diesel-hydraulic 2,200hp Type 4 No.D862 *'Viking', seen* returning to Plymouth with the 3.40pm milk empties from Wood Lane. The NBL/MAN built batch, in all totalling thirty three, had scandalously short working lives - a whisker off ten years each on average. Rounding errors in the conversion process from metric to imperial measurements when the MAN drawings were received by NBL contributed greatly to inferior tolerances in the finished engines in these machines, which in turn resulted in poor reliability.

Opposite bottom - The electrification of the West Coast Main Line to London and subsequent extensive disruption this caused required alternative arrangements to be made to cover the period whilst the work was carried out. Several diversionary routes were introduced to compensate, one being a direct service between Birkenhead and Paddington via Birmingham. When the engineering work were completed in March 1967 an all new electric service between Wolverhampton Low Level and Euston was introduced, the service over the old GWR line to Birkenhead being withdrawn. During the period of work Brush diesel-electric 2,750hp Type 4 No.D1731 passes Hanger Lane on 9 October 1965 with the 07.40 Birkenhead Woodside-Paddington. *The late Andrew Smith / authors collection*

Above - The 1955 Modernisation Plan envisaged the provision of single car DMU units to replace the GWR built railcars then operating on Western Region branch lines. In 1958 the first batch, Nos. W55000-19, were constructed by the Gloucester Railway Carriage & Wagon Company. Tow years later in 1960 and following on from the success with the Gloucesters, a further sixteen single cars were built, this time by Pressed Steel at their Linwood plant in Scotland, they were allocated the numbers W55020-35 These later cars were easily distinguishable by the roof mounted headcode box, and 'antler' like exhaust pipes. As previously, non-powered driving trailers were also constructed, again to provide extra capacity when needed. These latter cars were originally numbered W56280-9. No. W55024 is seen at Drayton Green Halt on a Greenford – Ealing Broadway service, augmented with a driving trailer. During the off-peaks the trailers were detached and left in the reversing siding at Ealing.   *The On Line Video collection*

As referred to briefly on the previous page, to give greater flexibility in the use of the new single car units at peak times, nine non-gangwayed driving trailers were built at the same time. Numbered W56291-9 they featured a driving cab at one end only. This early 1960s view shows single unit W55013, strengthened by the addition of a driving trailer, pausing at Drayton Green Halt on the Ealing Broadway – Greenford branch. The rural feel, epitomised by the GWR pagoda shelter, defies belief that this is in fact a West London suburb. In the background are seen two sides of the triangle allowing trains to join / leave the main Paddington - Reading route in either direction.

The On Line Video collection

Swindon built Warship diesel-hydraulic 2,200hp Type 4 No.D819 'Goliath' hurries out through the West London suburbs at Southall on Sunday 2 May 1965 with the 17.35 Paddington to Taunton service. There is little doubt that the machines equipped with Maybach engines achieved better results than their North British MAN counterparts, but these were obtained at an annual cost well in excess of their diesel-electric equivalents, which did little to quell growing disquiet at Marylebone about the merits of the hydraulics. Leaving Paddington with a North British example with MAN engines, often required all windows and doors open to let out the smoke and exhaust fumes that came in through every crevice. It was considered that if Old Oak was passed without incident there was a reasonable chance of completing the journey! *Brain Dale*

Right - The 101-strong class of Beyer Peacock 'Hymek' diesel-hydraulic 1,700hp locomotives to Type 3 specification was a joint venture with Stone-Platt Industries and Armstrong Siddeley Ltd. The 16-cylinder Maybach MD870, manufactured under licence by Siddeley, was the largest engine used in the hydraulics. The sleek ultra-modern appearance, which rivalled that of the 'Westerns', was produced by design consultants Wilkes & Ashmore. No.D7056 in the original elaborate livery of Brunswick green, with lime green relief along the bottom of the bodywork, and window surrounds in ivory white, is outside Southall shed on 5 December 1965. When repainted into rail blue, No.D7056 only received the small yellow warning panel, not the full yellow end. *Brian Dale*

Bottom right - The Western Region management, always keen to retain a degree of autonomy, named sixteen of their Brush diesel-electric 2,750hp Type 4 locomotives during 1965-66. Most received names representing figures of strength and power associated with ancient mythologies, the remainder with a GWR theme. On 11 May 1974 the former No. D1666 '*Odin*', re-numbered as 47.081 under the TOPS scheme, hurries through Hayes & Harlington heading a Harwich Parkeston Quay – Hinksey Freightliner. The art-deco style factory buildings on the left belong to the EMI group. *Pat Avery*

To celebrate the Golden Jubilee of The Institution of Locomotive Engineers in May 1961, an exhibition was held at Marylebone goods depot. Amongst the twenty locomotives on display was the last steam locomotive built by BR, 9F 2-10-0 No.92220 'Evening Star', and the world record holder for steam, ex-LNER A4 No.60022 'Mallard'. On the 12 May His Royal Highness, The Duke of Edinburgh, was the distinguished guest at this event, during which he named an immaculate Warship diesel-hydraulic locomotive 2,200hp Type 4 No.D.829 'Magpie'. After the visit Prince Philip returned to Windsor by special train directly from the goods depot. For most of the relatively short journey he drove the diesel, under supervision from Driver Fred Mason, seen here at Windsor & Eton Central after arrival.   *Noodle Books collection*

Forerunners of the first generation diesel multiple units were the outstandingly successful Great Western Railway built railcars, which transformed previously loss-making branch services whilst retaining the ability to perform fast express work when required. Southall maintained a healthy quota of these cars, primarily for local service work on London area branch lines which proved ideal territory. The last examples remained until August 1962, when sufficient numbers of new BR units had arrived so making them redundant.

Railcar W21W, displaying a red and cream livery, is one of the later 'non-streamlined' members of the class equipped with beefier AEC engines thus capable of hauling a trailing load, seen at West Drayton & Yiewsley on 31 July 1958 sporting the well suited carmine and cream livery. West Drayton was the junction for both Uxbridge Vine Street and Staines West branches, closed to passengers in 1962 and 1965 respectively.

The late Andrew Smith / authors collection

Here the same unit is seen at Staines West, the angular appearance displayed to advantage, dated perhaps now but still considered relatively modern in the 1960s. The first units of the type had been introduced by the GWR in the 1930s and were intended as a fast shuttle between important main line destinations, Birmingham and Cradiff being one such working. These first cars were not fitted for multiple working although passenger comfort was considered a priority and they were equipped with buffet facilities. Unfortunately their very popularity meant not all intending passengers could be accommodated and revision was quickly made to a locomotive hauled set - thus defeating the object. The next stage was diesel 'No. 18', a prototype car capable of hauling a trailing load. This proved its worth on the Lambourn branch hauling occasional horse-boxes or a strengthening coach at peak times. Even so the technology was being pushed to the limit and it was not uncommon for one of the two engines to fail resulting in the a limp home at reduced speed with an array of discarded engine components collected from the trackside in a bucket.

The late Andrew Smith / authors collection

Complete with 'speed whiskers' - the latter intended as a means of identifying the approach to men walking on the track - an unidentified railcar runs across the complex of trackwork at Southall. The BR multiple unit 'green' livery suited the vehicles well. It was perhaps fortunate that none survived long enough to appear in blue / grey!

The On Line Video collection

Top left and right - The final batch of railcars built to GWR design were Nos.35 to 38, designed as twin-coupled units complete with buffets and toilets for working an extended capacity Birmingham to Cardiff express service. With driving compartments situated at the outer ends of the set, seating capacity was 104, increasing to 184 if a standard coach was coupled between the cars. Unfortunately No.37 was fire damaged beyond repair in 1947, leading to a rebuild of railcar No.W33W in 1954 for use with No.38. The later pairing is alongside Southall shed on 31 May 1960, sporting the final livery of BR multiple unit green with 'speed whiskers'. Lining up with the twin-set is a trio of 'non-streamlined' cars in the earlier carmine and cream colours. *The late Andrew Smith/authors collection*

Right - No.W21W receives the nearest equivalent to a hand valet from the cleaners outside Southall shed on 29 September 1958.

The late Andrew Smith / authors collection

LONDON MIDLAND REGION

In the autumn of 1967 major resignalling and track alterations at Paddington meant Birmingham trains were diverted to use Marylebone as their London terminus. This briefly brought about a renaissance of main line motive power over the former Great Central line and was a welcome interlude from the otherwise usual diet of suburban DMU's. 'Warship' hauled trains tended to be of the North British built batch (D833-867), but on the odd occasion a Swindon built example would appear, as here when maroon liveried 'No.D808' Centaur was photographed preparing to head north with 1M11, the diverted 08.15 service to Birmingham New Street.

The On Line Video collection.

Completed in late 1967, HS4000 'Kestrel' was a private venture by Brush Engineering Loughborough, in association with Sulzer Bros Ltd, to design and build a locomotive that met the revised specification for Type 5 locomotives regarding weight and power.

The principle was that a single 4,000hp engine would require less maintenance than the comparable twin-engined machines then in use, also that the power output available would render double heading of freight trains obsolete.

On Monday 29 January 1968 HS4000 is seen at Marylebone in preparation for the official handing over ceremony and return test run to Princes Risborough. Interestingly the number was an anachronism of the Brush parent company Hawker Siddeley (HS), and the engine's power output (4,000). After extensive testing BR decided not to pursue the project further, and in 1971 Kestrel was sold to the USSR. *Noodle Books collection*.

Left - On 20 August 1966 a commendably clean Birmingham RCW 1,250hp Type 2, No.D5407 shunts coal empties at Neasden South Junction. Cricklewood depot had received a substantial allocation of these locomotives in 1962, at that time intended for use on cross-London freight services as well as St.Pancras -Tilbury boat trains. The gradual decline of both businesses eventually led to the entire class being reallocated to Scotland during 1969. In turn this was part of a replacement programme that allowed withdrawal of the less successful centre cab Clayton diesels.

The late Andrew Smith / authors collection

Above - Derby built Diesel Multiple Units were progressively introduced to Marylebone outer suburban services from 1961. Here a standard 4-car unit, Motor Brake Second M51879 leading, comes off the High Wycombe line at Neasden South Junction on 20 August 1966 with the 10.00 from Princes Risborough. Neasden power station, commissioned by the Metropolitan Railway in 1904, can be seen in the background behind the Underground depot. This power station, which along with Lots Road at Chelsea supplied the entire London Transport network, ceased generating in 1968.

The late Andrew Smith / authors collection

On 3 September 1966, the last day of through trains over the former Great Central main line, BR Sulzer 1,100hp Type 2 No.D5089, powers away from Harrow-on-the-Hill with the final 08.15 Nottingham Victoria – Marylebone service. Punctuality towards the end was far from exemplary, and true to form, this train was running over an hour late after the failure of Stanier Class 5 No. 44872 at Aylesbury, resulting in the diesel substitution. The last rites on the GC were administered in the early hours of the following day, when No.D5089 was in action again hauling the overnight train from Manchester from Woodford Halse to its destination at Marylebone.

The late Andrew Smith / authors collection

'The Caledonian' was introduced by the London Midland Region in June 1957as an additional Anglo-Scottish service to rival that of the Eastern Region's 'Talisman' service. The initial point-to-point timing of 6 hours 40 minutes each way with a solitary stop at Carlisle proved popular, but preparations for electrification, together with the introduction of additional stops, meant considerable increases in timings, and were met with a poor public response. In this June 1963 view at Euston, English Electric 2,000hp Type 4 No.D299 is at the head of the 3.45pm departure north. Of note is the distinctive headboard which featured the Scottish Saltire and the English cross of St.George. Among the train spotters on the platform are those sporting satchels, shorts and sandals; *de rigueur* for the period.

Keith Jones

The evening shadows lengthen at Euston as English Electric 2,700hp Type 4 demonstrator No. DP2 in its familiar 'Deltic' body-shell, marshals stock ahead of the 7.30pm departure to Inverness, The engine will work the train as far as Crewe. A true pioneer, DP2 was constructed in response to prototypes on offer from both Brush and Birmingham Railway Carriage & Wagon Co. As such it would lead to the second generation Type 4 specification requirements of British Rail, albeit in a differing body shell, and would subsequently pave the way for the fifty Class 50 locomotives constructed as the pre electrification stop gap motive power to operate between the North West and Glasgow. Entering service in May 1962 at Camden shed, DP2 worked on the London Midland Region for a year before moving to Finsbury Park where it was allocated to the Deltic pool. Unfortunately DP2 met an abrupt end on the 31 July 1967, colliding at high speed with a derailed freight train near Thirsk when working the 12:00 Kings Cross - Edinburgh Waverley service. Regrettably seven passengers were killed in the incident. Damaged beyond repair DP2 was eventually returned to the English Electric works at Newton-le Willows where it was scrapped in 1968. (In the same way that the number HS4000 was an anachronism for the maker and power output, so DP2 stood for 'Diesel Prototype No. 2.' 'Diesel prototype No. 1' had been the pre-production 'Deltic' of 1955 although in this earlier case no actual number was carried.)
Noodle Books collection.

Left - Dubbed the 'Ivatt Twins' after designer H.G.Ivatt, the London Midland & Scottish Railway diesel pioneers Nos.10000 and 10001, were at the forefront of main line diesel traction development in this country. First to enter service in December 1947 just a few weeks before nationalisation, was No.10000, sister locomotive No.10001 following in July 1948. Each was powered by a single 16SVT 1,600hp engine, this and the transmission supplied by English Electric as their contribution to this joint venture with the LMS. Presented from new in a striking black livery with polished aluminium waistband lining and raised numerals, both locomotives acquired standard Brunswick Green livery in 1956 and later received the addition of small yellow warning panels. In this final guise No.10001 is seen inside the roundhouse at Willesden shed on 14 February 1965. Uncertainty as to whether this fine machine might become a candidate for preservation meant a two year stay of execution from the cutters' torch after withdrawal in March 1966. Regretfully it was all to no avail, as the appointed hour finally arrived at nearby Cox & Danks, North Acton in February 1968. *Brian Dale*

Above - Lurking inside Willesden shed roundhouse on 14 February 1965, and the sole example of the 10-strong class to be allocated to the London area of the LM region for any appreciable length of time, is Hudswell-Clarke diesel-mechanical 0-6-0 shunter No. D2518. Although quite stylish, these off-centre cab shunters ranked amongst the pilot scheme's most short-lived types, all having being withdrawn by the end of 1967, a mere six years after introduction.

Brian Dale

Left - The closure of so many local and rural lines as a result of the Beeching cuts meant that there was an ever increasing surplus of DMUs. In this September 1967 view a cascaded Derby Lightweight 2-car unit eases into Platform 10 at Watford Junction with the 14.27 service from St.Albans Abbey. Although highly successful when compared with other early prototypes, this class of DMU had all been withdrawn by the end of 1969. The remnants of Watford shed, which closed in March 1965, is in the background. The white buildings beyond the railway boundary belonged to Fishburn Inks, a name synonymous with Watford as a major printing town at the time.

Pat Avery

This page, top - The West Coast Main Line had been starved of investment for years, with resultant poor quality track work and lower line speeds in comparison to the East Coast route. Unable to sustain high speed output for lengthy periods, the English Electric 2,000hp Type 4 diesels had been shunned by the Eastern Region, but when transferred to the London Midland were welcomed and quickly settled down as the preferred motive power choice for principal expresses prior to electrification. Heading through the north-west London suburbs is No.D302, accelerating past South Kenton with the 13.00 Euston-Glasgow Central *Mid-day Scot.* In common with other daytime named trains the relatively light eight coach formations were seat reservation only; standing passengers not being permitted.

Noodle Books collection.

This page, bottom - The Midland Pullman was introduced in July 1960 as a luxury first-class service aimed at the high end of the Manchester-London business market disaffected by electrification work then in progress on the West Coast Main Line. On 1 April 1966 under Barlow's magnificent trainshed roof at St.Pancras, one of the pair of six-car Blue Pullman diesel-electric units used on the service is waiting to depart with the 18.20 return to Manchester, Motor Brake First M60091 leading. The Blue Pullman trains were replaced by the electric loco-hauled 'Manchester Pullman' running from Manchester Piccadilly to Euston a fortnight later, this change also marked the end of the Midland Main Line as the premier route between the two cities.

The late Andrew Smith / authors collection

Above - In advance of impending electrification some of the local Euston-Northampton workings were converted to diesel haulage from November 1959. Idling at Euston between these duties in the summer of 1960 was BR/Sulzer diesel-electric 1,160hp Type 2 No.D5018, prior to the addition of electrification 'flashes' and small yellow warning panels. Interestingly this was one of the class members equipped with 'Athermos' pressure-lubricated plain bearing axle boxes, instead of the usual roller bearing type. *Julian Bowden*

Opposite page, bottom - Moments after leaving the extensive sidings at Brent, the 18.04 inter-regional freight to Feltham of 20 July 1965, headed by Birmingham Railway Carriage & Wagon Co diesel-electric 1,550hp Type 3 No.D6544, eases up alongside Brent No.2's home signal. Ahead lays a leisurely evening meander through the West London suburbs via the Dudding Hill Line, Acton and Kew East Junction. The coaling tower on the extreme right marks the location of the former Cricklewood steam shed complex, which closed in December 1964.

The late Andrew Smith / authors collection

Above - The suburban services from Moorgate / St Pancras to Bedford moved to diesel multiple unit operation from January 1960. However the first few months proved problematical, with necessary steam or diesel substitutions hauling conventional coaching stock a frequent occurrence. Consequently this transitional period on the former Midland main line resulted in numerous unusual workings; one oddity produced was Metropolitan-Vickers Co-Bo diesel-electric 1,200hp Type 2 No. D5714, in original form with wrap around cab windows, seen here passing the site of the disused Finchley Road station on a Bedford bound local service. For a few months that year Cricklewood depot had the final seven members of the class, Nos. D5713-19, on their allocation for use on the overnight 'Condor' express freight services between Hendon and Glasgow. An appalling reliability record meant that availability was often as low as fifteen per cent and by the autumn all had been moved on, their relatively brief sojourn in the capital at an end.

The On Line Video collection

Left - On Sunday 30 May 1965, a 1959 built Derby 4-car suburban diesel multiple unit slows for the stop at Mill Hill Broadway with a St.Pancras-Luton local. Over on the down fast line an unidentified Birmingham RC&W Co. Type 2 can be seen commandeered for engineers' line occupation duties. These high density units, equipped with Rolls Royce engines and torque converter transmissions were used intensively and generally gave good service. Unfortunately the fleet was also beset with failures of various kinds, notably a series of disastrous fires, the most serious of which resulted in severe injuries and in two instances fatalities, many passengers having to jump hurriedly from blazing vehicles. The cause of these catastrophic events was found to be drive shaft failure puncturing fuel tanks, the flammable liquid contents subsequently igniting. The fire record of under-floor engined diesel multiple units on British Rail was not good, particularly when compared with that of the diesel-electric multiple-units then operating on the Southern Region.

Brian Dale

Left - Unofficially nicknamed 'Rats' due to their high build numbers and common sightings in and around the London area on just about any permutation of work one could think of, was the highly versatile BR/Sulzer diesel-electric Type 2. The final variant, constructed between 1961 and 1967, had an uprated 6DLA28-B 1,250hp engine and redesigned bodywork. This bodywork change principally meant that the gangway doors were omitted and the location of the air intakes moved from the body sides to above the cantrail. Additionally roof mounted four character headcode boxes were provided at each end replacing the folding discs fitted to earlier examples. Designated Class 25 under the TOPS renumbering system of 1973 and typical of the rail blue period, is air-braked No.25.205, the erstwhile D7555, seen at St.Albans City with an Up parcels service to St.Pancras, 30 June 1979.

Pat Avery

The new order rubs shoulders with the old guard outside Willesden motive power depot in 1965; respectively Pilot scheme English Electric 1,000hp Type 1 No.D8012, along with Stanier Class 2-6-4T No.42577. After Devons Road Bow diesel depot closed in February 1964, No.D8012, along with the other eighteen class members allocated there were either transferred here, or to 30A Stratford.

Saturday afternoon spotters watch on at Euston as prototype LMS/English Electric 1,600hp No.10001 is opened up in preparation for the ascent of Camden Bank on 22 March 1958 with a Bletchley local. Originally intended for main line use, Nos. 10000 and 10001 were meant to be compared directly with the final two Stanier Pacifics, Nos 46256/7. Working in multiple the two diesels were certainly a match and of course with far little effort on the part of the crew. As time progressed however, the diesels were used more singly leaving steam to reign supreme. In their later years their work was confined to local duties.

The late Andrew Smith / authors collection

Attracting attention from rain coated admirers at Euston on Saturday 22 March 1958 is Southern Region built 2,000hp diesel-electric No.10203, seen after arrival from Glasgow Central with the up 'Royal Scot'. The increased power output available in comparison to the earlier prototype build diesels of LMS and Southern origin, Nos. 10000/1 and 10201/2 respectively, meant that No.10203 was capable of hauling the heavy Anglo-Scottish expresses single handed. However the limelight was quickly captured on these services by the newly introduced English Electric Type 4's from autumn 1958 onwards, and No.10203, along with the other Ivatt and Bulleid designed quartet, found ever dwindling use and by 1966 all had been withdrawn.

The late Andrew Smith / authors collection

The first batch of English Electric 1,000hp Type 1's, introduced in 1957, were allocated to Devons Road at Bow to work cross-London transfer freights and where they were evaluated against the contemporary North British and British Thomson-Houston designs. The failure of these competitors to provide anything resembling reliable locomotives in this power range meant that the 'choppers' became an easy choice for the British Transport Commission when deciding standard production requirements. One of the early prototypes, No.D8005, is at the nearby Bow works on 6 September 1958. This former North London Railway facility undertook heavy repairs to diesels based at Devons Road until 1960, when the work was transferred to Derby.

The late Andrew Smith / authors collection

Sunday slumber at Willesden MPD on 9 November 1958 for Stratford based interloper British Thomson-Houston diesel-electric 800hp Type 1 No.D8206. A total of 44 of these Bo-Bo diesel locomotives were built powered by a Paxman 16 cylinder engine. Four electric traction motors transferred the power to the axles. Although slightly lighter than the EE type seem above, 68 tons against 72 tons, any advantage gained was lost in the 20% reduction in engine power provided. Similarly the tractive effort at the rail was a poor 37,500 lbs against the EE 42,000 lbs.

The late Andrew Smith / authors collection

One of the attractively designed British Thomson-Houston 800 hp Type 1 diesel-electrics, No.D8201, is between duties at Devons Road Bow on 6 September 1958. Badly damaged by heavy bombing during the Blitz, Devons Road had been rebuilt by the London Midland & Scottish Railway after the war and was subsequently converted by their successors British Railways into a dedicated diesel maintenance depot. Unfortunately the steady shift of freight traffic to the road network, together with the rundown of the London docks system to eventual extinction meant an oversupply of locomotives with diminishing workloads and as a result this depot closed in February 1964.

The late Andrew Smith / authors collection

At Watford Junction on 21 April 1957 is the prototype Motor Brake Second
M79742M. With a driving compartment provided at each end, and seating for 28,
the car weighed in at an economical 15 tons. Power was provided by an AEC
6-cylinder engine producing 125 hp, badged for British United Traction (B.U.T),
driving a mechanical cardan shaft and flywheel transmission to a four speed
epicyclic gearbox and further cardan shaft to final drive.

The late Andrew Smith / authors collection

In 1952 Associated Commercial Vehicles / British United Traction ventured into the lightweight railcar market constructing a prototype three car
4-wheel railbus unit. Bodywork was by Park Royal Vehicles with engines provided by AEC. Both organisations being part of the ACV / BUT group.
This demonstrator, painted two-tone grey with red lining and made up of a Motor Brake Second, Motor Second and Trailer Second, was extensively
trialled throughout the country and purchased by British Railways the following year. In 1955 five similar cars were built with three more following in
1957. The three prototypes could be distinguished from the production units by their half-drop windows and lower skirt panels (later removed),
whereas the later build had sliding windows without skirts. All eleven cars, mockingly referred to as 'Flying Brick's' due to their angular box-like
appearance were later repainted into BR green livery. All had been withdrawn from service by 1962.

Although largely remembered for working Watford Junction-St.Albans Abbey services, the 'Flying Brick's' did appear periodically on the short branch line between Harrow & Wealdstone and Belmont. Here a two car unit arrives at the latter station on 12 July 1958. Despite enjoying reasonably healthy commuter traffic to Euston via Harrow, the off-peak loadings were light, resulting in a closure recommendation in the Beeching report. Despite vigorous protests the end finally came in early October 1964 - one of the few London area lines to lose its passenger service.

The late Andrew Smith / authors collection

A three car unit, with one of the prototype Motor Second cars leading, arrives at St.Albans Abbey on 21 April 1957. Almost one hundred years earlier both the London & North Western and Great Northern had opened separate branch lines to St.Albans: from Watford Junction and Hatfield respectively. The extensive sidings to the right served the city gas works visible in the background, which was supplied by two coal trains per day over the former GN route, although the shunt engine came over daily from Watford shed. The impressive gantry in the foreground signalled left to right, GN bay to Watford Junction, LNW platform to Hatfield and LNW platform to Watford Junction. Following severe rationalisation in the 1960s, this scene is now unrecognisable.

The late Andrew Smith / authors collection

The close proximity of Marylebone Goods Depot to BRB headquarters made it an ideal location for exhibitions and demonstrations in the years that followed the announcement of the modernisation programme. One interesting development, intended to increase the competitiveness of rail freight services, was the appearance of the Roadrailer, an idea pioneered in the USA by the Chesapeake & Ohio Railroad. It was an experimental dual-purpose vehicle designed to travel on rail or road, the concept of which was to use an articulated road trailer fitted with two axles at the rear, one with rail, the other road wheels. The axles were carried on a frame pivoted at the centre enabling either set of wheels to be lifted clear, leaving the other pair to carry the vehicle. The front end of the trailer was supported by the road tractor unit, or on a purpose built four wheeled wagon, the rear of the trailer being fitted with a coupling to connect to the wagon behind.   The trailers were constructed in the UK by Pressed Steel in a joint venture with British Railways and British Road Services. In the late summer of 1960 two prototype Roadrailers were used in a demonstration at Marylebone that used a British Road Services Bristol HA6L tractor unit, and Cricklewood allocated diesel-electric 350hp shunter No.D3869, coupled to a four wheeled adaptor wagon. Despite vigorous marketing to users and road operators the idea was not successful, mainly because of the time taken to assemble and re-assemble the train at either end of the journey. The project was finally abandoned when the Freightliner intermodal container system was launched in 1965. *The On Line Video collection*

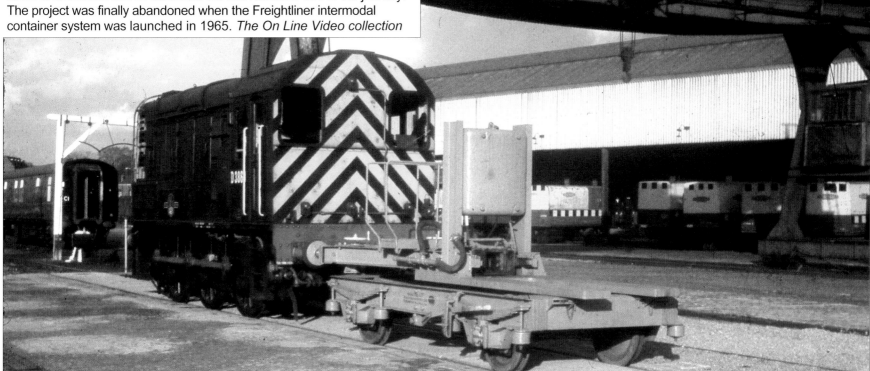

EASTERN REGION

On a warm summer evening in July 1969 Deltic diesel-electric 3,300hp Type 5 No.D9006 'The Fife and Forfar Yeomanry' gets under way from Kings Cross with 1L34, the 17.30 'Yorkshire Pullman' to Leeds, Bradford and Harrogate. The smart rake of Metro-Cammell Pullman cars behind the Deltic, the last to be built in umber and cream livery, was based on the British Railways Mark 1 design and fitted with Commonwealth bogies, making them suitable for 100mph running. Despite this bold attempt to modernise premier East Coast Main Line services patronage steadily declined, due in part to the development of the motorway network and increasing competition from domestic air travel. These elegant vehicles did however linger on for another decade until withdrawal in 1978.

The Kings Cross area. before the 1977 improvement project known as 'clearing the throat' was an enigma. The original Great Northern Railway arrival and departure train sheds were not well suited to the meteoric passenger traffic increase caused by the rapid development of North London suburbs in the late nineteenth and early twentieth centuries, which together with the adjoining suburban local station, opened in 1874 and enlarged in 1895 and 1924 respectively, ended up an untidy mess. Emerging from these dreary and drab environs on 21 August 1965 was a very smart looking Brush diesel-electric 1,470hp Type 2 No.D5672, heading a semi-fast service to Baldock. To the right of the locomotive is the steep 1 in 49 gradient from the Metropolitan Widened Lines. The Dickensian wooden sleepered Platform 16, commonly referred to as Hotel Curve, only added to the distinct air of neglect in this part of the station. To witness the re-start of a Brush Type 2 on this incline with a fully loaded evening commuter train from Moorgate had to be seen and heard to be believed.

Brian Dale

Left - The limited week-end lunch time peak trains from Moorgate harked back to the days when offices in the City of London opened on a Saturday morning. Whereas the Monday to Friday service was a mixture of loco hauled stock and diesel multiple units, those on Saturday's were exclusively Cravens 2-car DMU's operating in tandem. On the left an empty working rattles through Barbican en-route to Moorgate on 30 October 1976, where it will form the penultimate midday service to Hertford North. On the right a brace of units, formed of Driving Trailer Composite E56429, Motor Brake Second E51471, Driving Trailer Composite E56447 and Motor Brake Second E51260, pause briefly whilst heading the Locomotive Club of Great Britain's Greater London & Southminster railtour

Pat Avery

Bottom - The subterranean environs of the City Widened Lines are immediately apparent as Brush diesel-electric 1,470hp Class 31 No.31.404, formerly No. D5605, eases away from Kings Cross LT station into the cavernous gloom of Clerkenwell tunnel with the 08.44 New Barnet – Moorgate commuter service on 22 October 1976. This peak hour route into the city from Hertfordshire ceased a fortnight later, replaced by Great Northern Electrics operating over the former Northern City Line from Finsbury Park to Moorgate.
All locomotives and diesel multiple units working over the Widened Lines were required to have tripcock equipment fitted, in order to be compatible with London Transport signalling when working into Moorgate. *Pat Avery*

The ubiquitous and versatile Brush / Sulzer 2,750hp diesel-electric Type 4s in all variations had a build strength totalling 512. Class leader was No. D1500, which entered service on the Eastern Region in September 1962. Later that year the locomotive was loaned to the Western for evaluation and trialling purposes culminating, in February 1963, with the impressive movement of a sixteen coach test train unaided from a standing start on Dainton Bank in South Devon, the third steepest main line gradient in Britain. After returning to the ER, D1500 is seen stabled alongside Finsbury Park No.2 signal box, in company with oil tanks destined for the diesel depot, situated out of sight behind the photographer.

The On Line Video collection

With a failure rate four times greater than that of comparable Type 2 specification motive power then operating on the Eastern Region, the ten strong 'Baby Deltic' class of 1,160hp diesel-electrics constructed by English Electric in 1959, were plagued with problems from the outset. British Railways initially refused to take delivery due to weight issues, mainly with the ancillary components fitted, resulting in drastic reduction measures being made in order to make the limit. When they did enter service persistent engine seizures and auxiliary gearbox failures blighted the entire fleet. As a consequence all were eventually withdrawn and returned to the manufacturer for extensive modification. During this refurbishment the opportunity was taken to revise the front end layout by removing the gangway doors and headcode discs as originally fitted, replacing these with a four character route indicator box, which also improved the appearance greatly. Despite the heavy costs incurred, paid for ultimately by the British taxpayer, the 1967 National Traction Plan identified the class for an early demise. The last survivor, No. D5905 withdrawn in 1971, was the sole example to appear in standard rail blue livery.

Contrasting 'Baby Deltic' design variation at Kings Cross; *above:* Heading for the suburban platforms on 21 August 1965 is No. D5906, in modified form and wearing the smart livery of two-tone green with small yellow warning panels. Ironically this was the first member of the class to be withdrawn in September 1968. *right:* When new, all locomotives were presented in standard green livery with grey sole bar, gangway doors and headcode discs, as portrayed by Hornsey allocated No. D5902 seen running into Platform 12 with an Up local service.

Brian Dale and Noodle Books collection

Kings Cross station throat in July 1969: for many these were the halcyon days of the diesel era and pure joy for the young spotter at the platform end. On the left a Finsbury Park stalwart, Brush diesel-electric 1,470hp Type 2 No.D5606, eases away from the steeply inclined Platform 16 and the City Widened lines with a Moorgate - Welwyn Garden City commuter service. Above the Brush is the wide cantilevered arm of signal KC220, its roller blind route indicator showing 'S', denoting down slow line through Gasworks Tunnel. Beyond, Deltic diesel-electric 3,300hp Type 5 No.D9019 'Royal Highland Fusilier' is on shed outside the 'Elephant House', having arrived earlier with the Up Tees Tyne Pullman. In the middle distance a Brush Type 4 arrives with non-gangwayed compartment stock.

To celebrate Her Royal Highness Queen Elizabeth's twenty-fifth anniversary as reigning monarch in 1977, British Rail rebranded the 07:45 King's Cross-Edinburgh and 15:00 return as 'The Silver Jubilee'. Booked for Deltic haulage throughout, inaugural services were launched on 8 June and operated until 30 December. On 4 August Class 55 No.55014 'The Duke of Wellingtons Regiment' replete with special headboard, had charge of 1S12, the northbound departure to 'Auld Reekie'.

The Brush diesel-electric Type 2's proved worthy successors to the ex-LNER B1 4-6-0 steam locomotives they replaced. On 18 March 1961 No. D5679 of the production build passes Copenhagen Junction signal box with an up local for Kings Cross. The signal gantry the train is passing underneath in this view was in fact controlled by Belle Isle Up cabin, out of picture.

The Transport Treasury

Deep in East End territory, North British 1,100hp Type 2 Bo-Bo No. D6114 is seen at Bromley Junction during the period of extensive electrification work on the former London Tilbury & Southend lines to and from Fenchurch Street. In this instance engineers' occupation of the adjoining District Lines was necessary for the erection of the overhead power masts, one of which is visible behind the locomotive. The severed tracks branching to the left were once the chord that connected the LT&S to the North London Railway at Bow. Plagued by an appalling record for unreliability and erratic performances, the NB Type 2s class struggled to perform in the capital. Matters had deteriorated to such an extent that by September 1960 BR migrated the entire Eastern Region allocation to Scotland. Operating closer to the NBL works in Glasgow meant that repair work could be carried out with less disruption elsewhere.

Pat Avery

Top - Box like and somewhat austere in appearance, the 800hp Type 1 locomotives Nos.D8400-9, built by the North British Locomotive Company in 1958 ranked amongst another of the worst of all pilot scheme diesel designs. No.D8401, seen here at Stratford, and the other nine class members, spent their working careers allocated to 30A, but frequent engine failures often accompanied by alarming pyrotechnic displays, meant that there was lengthy periods spent lying idle. This reputation for unreliability rendered them obsolete by the autumn of 1968.

The On Line Video collection

Bottom - By comparison, and in common with a number of other pilot scheme diesels, the English Electric 1,750hp Type 3s entered revenue earning service on the Great Eastern section of the Eastern Region, where they were quick to settled down on both passenger or freight work. Here at Stratford the doyen of the class, No. D6700, is pictured prior to the introduction of yellow warning panels. The design also shows the family resemblance to the larger English Electric Type 4s.

The On Line Video collection

Opposite page - In response to increasing numbers of trackside fatalities due to unseen green liveried diesels blending into the landscape, the Eastern Region selected two Brush 1,250hp Type 2 machines, Nos.D5578/9, to be outshopped from new in 'chromatic blue' and 'golden ochre' liveries respectively for evaluation purposes. The authorities had intended to display both machines in a blaze of publicity at Liverpool Street on 16 January 1960, but in the event only No.D5579 appeared: No.D5578 had failed its acceptance trials at Doncaster works prior to delivery. A few months later in May 1960 and with matters resolved, D5578 is at Stratford in the experimental blue colour whilst also sporting red bufferbeams and a black roof. Of note are the blue star coupling codes that matched the main body colour, picked out with white circular background as relief. A repaint to standard green with small yellow warning panels occurred in May 1964, No. D5579 following suit in late 1966.

In 1956 the Lincoln based firm of Ruston & Hornsby constructed two diesel-mechanical 165hp shunters, Nos. D2957-8, to a 0-4-0 wheel configuration for use in the docks at Immingham. Within a year they had both gone to Stratford, replacing the diminutive ex-Great Eastern Railway tanks of 1914 vintage that had worked in the yards and wharves and were suitable only for shunting by small four-wheeled locomotives, such as the Pepper Warehouses in East India Dock at Canning Town. This work evaporated after the docks closed in 1966; the pair being withdrawn by 1968. In more productive times No.D2957 is seen at Stratford in-between duties.

The Transport Treasury

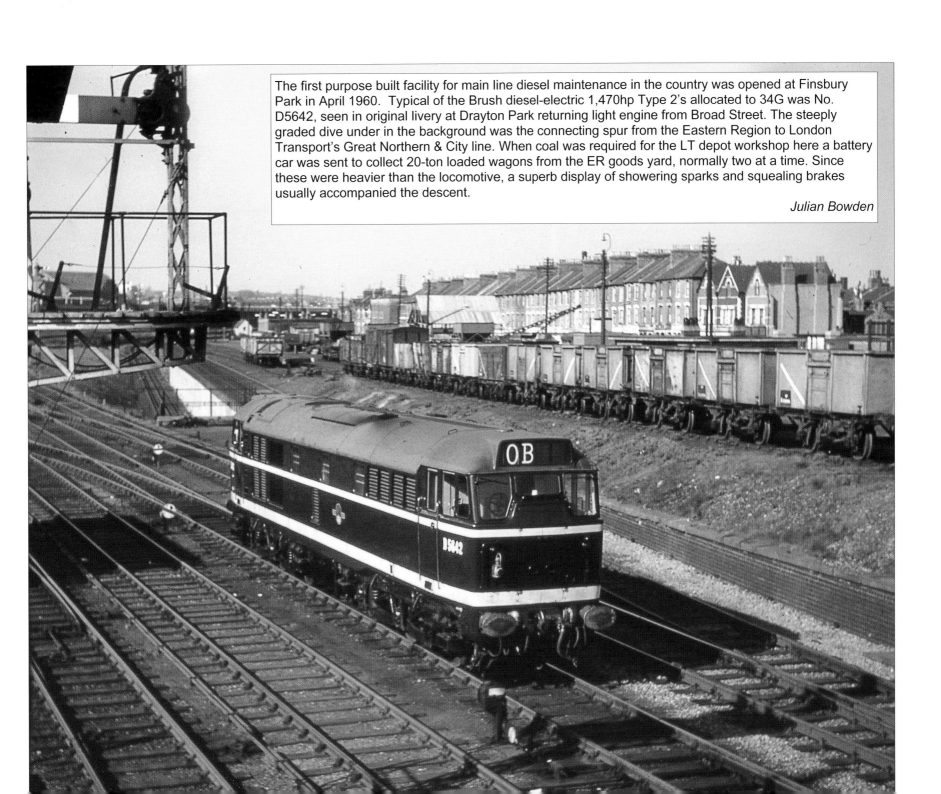

The first purpose built facility for main line diesel maintenance in the country was opened at Finsbury Park in April 1960. Typical of the Brush diesel-electric 1,470hp Type 2's allocated to 34G was No. D5642, seen in original livery at Drayton Park returning light engine from Broad Street. The steeply graded dive under in the background was the connecting spur from the Eastern Region to London Transport's Great Northern & City line. When coal was required for the LT depot workshop here a battery car was sent to collect 20-ton loaded wagons from the ER goods yard, normally two at a time. Since these were heavier than the locomotive, a superb display of showering sparks and squealing brakes usually accompanied the descent.

Julian Bowden

This page, top - Alongside Stratford depot in original Brunswick Green livery is BTH diesel-electric 800hp Type 1 No.D8215. In common with other casualties of the National Traction Plan cull, these diesels had remarkably short careers, withdrawals starting as early as April 1968, the last few lingering on in service until March 1971. However four class members, Nos.D8203/33/37/43, escaped the cutters' torch and were converted into non-powered train heating units: renumbered as ADB968000-3, at British Rail Engineering Ltd Doncaster. This process involved the removal of the traction motors and other non-essential equipment, the power plant still feeding the generator which was then used to provide an electrical supply to heat coaching stock.

The On Line Video collection

This page, bottom - "Where are the Hoods"? was the enquiry made by an American when train spotting at Liverpool Street in mid 1971. He had been referring to the D8200 class British Thompson-Houston diesel-electric 800hp Type 1 locomotives, but was too late. They had all gone. Troubled by design problems, notably engines that required excessive maintenance and a cab positioned part way down the body like a North American road switcher but giving the crew poor visibility in both directions of travel, doomed them to an early demise as soon as the 1967 National Traction Plan was in place. Withdrawn No .D8205 waits at Stratford depot for the final trip to the cutters' torch at Cohen's Kettering, in April 1969.

Pat Avery

Opposite - Early attempts at maintaining diesel locomotives at steam sheds such as Hornsey proved troublesome. It was quickly realised that the finer tolerances required for effective servicing meant that the 'clean room' environment was absolutely essential. For this purpose dedicated depots were built, with those at Devons Road Bow and Finsbury Park among the best known examples. Unsurprisingly Stratford was also equipped with good facilities; receiving attention on 21 June 1958 is 'Toffee-apple' Brush diesel-electric 1,250hp Type 2 No.D5507. The 'Toffee Apple' nickname coming from the shape of the main controller handle.

The late Andrew Smith / authors collection

The summer only Liverpool Street to Clacton Butlins Express ran from the late fifties to the mid-sixties. When diesel hauled, a distinctive circular yellow headboard with black lettering was used, as carried by Brush 1,250hp Type 2 No. D5509 seen getting under way for the Essex coast resort on Saturday 21 June 1958. A young spotter looks on, apparently finding the cameraman of greater interest!

The late Andrew Smith / authors collection

When photographed at Liverpool Street on 29 July 1958, Brush diesel-electric 1,250hp Type 2 No. D5513 had served less than two weeks in service, but would eventually go on to notch up a twenty year career, all of them based at Stratford.

The late Andrew Smith / authors collection

The first twenty four diesel-mechanical 204hp 0-6-0 shunters constructed by the Hunslet Engine Company between 1955-57 were allocated, with two exceptions, to East Anglian sheds and initially numbered in the series 11136-11176. These distinctive machines were retrospectively renumbered D2550-D2573 from mid-1958 onwards. In June that year No.11163 of Ipswich was in Stratford Works for attention, re-emerging as D2560.

The late Andrew Smith / authors collection

In February 1961 Birmingham Railway Carriage & Wagon Co diesel-electric 1,550hp Type 3 No. D6504 was sent on temporary loan to Finsbury Park from Hither Green. Starting on the 14 February, two consecutive overnight return trips were made between Hornsey and Edinburgh to test electric train heating equipment. Here the locomotive and seven coach rake prepares to leave Ferme Park on the inaugural run to Craigentinny. After the trials were concluded No. D6504 quickly returned to the Southern Region.

Noodle Books collection

Left - Possibly the smartest looking, if not the most reliable, four wheel railbuses were the two produced by the Bristol / Eastern Coach Works partnership in 1958. After completion at the ECW works in Lowestoft, the pair ran independently under their own power to Scotland, where they were used initially on the Speyside and Beith branch lines. Limited use led to a relatively short career, both being withdrawn in October 1966. On Sunday 24 August 1958, the only occasion either was seen in London, SC79958 is at Stratford during a lay-over stop en-route north to its working home of the border.

The late Andrew Smith / authors collection

Bottom - The Upminster to Grays branch first saw diesel multiple units in September 1956. As in steam days certain trains were extended to, or originated from, Tilbury Riverside, thus providing a ferry connection to Gravesend south of the Thames. On Wednesday 30 July 1958 a Derby Lightweight 2-car unit in BR green with 'speed whiskers', comprising Motor Brake Second E79039 and Driving Trailer E79255, pauses briefly at Grays with a Tilbury Riverside – Upminster service.

The late Andrew Smith / authors collection

Designed by Oliver Bulleid before nationalisation for use on the Southern Railway's non-electrified routes, the somewhat austere and box-like prototype diesel-electric 1,750hp D16/2 No. 10202, seen here at Waterloo, first emerged in September 1951 working alongside sister locomotive No.10201. A third locomotive with increased power output, No. 10203, materialised in 1954. After extensive use on the Southern the trio were transferred to the London Midland Region in 1955 working alongside ex-LMS pioneers Nos.10000/1. Increasingly side-lined by the production batch of English Electric built Type 4's introduced from 1958 onwards; this quintet was relegated from express passenger to mundane local work and freight duties. Withdrawn from service in 1963 breaking up eventually took place at Cashmore's Great Bridge in May 1968.

Noodle Books collection

In September 1963 control of the ex-LSWR lines west of Salisbury passed from the Southern to the Western Region. The Beeching Report published earlier that year had concluded that only one route was needed from London to the West Country and it came as no surprise when Western Region management announced that the one they wanted to discard belonged to their former adversary. Rumours of complete closure were rife, but in the end severe rationalisation of both line and infrastructure between Wilton, the new regional boundary, and Exeter narrowly avoided this becoming a reality. Diesel replaced steam from August 1964 onwards, although the questionable reliability of the 'Warship' class locomotives used as motive power added to the general frustration and decline in passenger traffic throughout the decade. Old rubs shoulders with new at Waterloo in 1965 – respectively rebuilt West Country 4-6-2 No.34036 'Westward Ho!' and, waiting to return westwards with a semi-fast service, Warship diesel-hydraulic 2,200hp Type 4 No.D811 'Daring'. In practice the Swindon built engines based at Newton Abbot, and later Laira, were generally used, but examples from the North British build did appear infrequently.

Julian Bowden

Under Southern auspices the 11.00 departure from Waterloo had traditionally been the prestigious 'Atlantic Coast Express', but after the September 1964 timetable recast by the Western Region was downgraded to an anonymous semi-fast service, as seen on 3 June 1967 when Newton Abbot based Warship diesel-hydraulic 2,200hp Type 4 No.D831 'Monarch' prepared to get under way westwards to Exeter. The additional stops, and lengthy single line sections beyond Salisbury, often the cause of frequent delays, led to considerable concern among passengers used to a far better standard. Modernisation on this route seen by passengers as regressive rather than progressive.

The late Andrew Smith / authors collection

Above - In the late 1950s the Southern Region designed an experimental dual powered locomotive equipped to operate from 750v dc third-rail collection, or from an on-board diesel engine so allowing use over non-electrified lines. The six prototypes Nos. E6001-6 and designated class 'JA', entered service from February 1962 onwards and were an instant success. Their versatility prompted SR management to order a further forty three locomotives, these being constructed by Vulcan Foundry between 1965-67. This later batch had modified traction motors which permitted a higher top speed of 90mph, resulting in the classification 'JB' - in order to make the distinction between the two variants. Less than a month into service 'JB' electro-diesel No. E6033 approaches Vauxhall with the 09.30 Waterloo-Bournemouth on 3 July 1966.

The late Andrew Smith / authors collection

Left - From the mid sixties onwards when rail blue with full yellow ends was adopted as standard livery, two Warship class diesel-hydraulics, Nos.D830 *'Majestic'*, and D831 *'Monarch'*, re-appeared after repaint but retaining the small yellow warning panels worn previously. From a distance this made the pair easily distinguishable, as this 3 June 1967 view at Waterloo shows when No.D831 *'Monarch'* mingled with Portsmouth line 4-COR electric units Nos. 3147 and 3131.

The late Andrew Smith / authors collection

Ably demonstrating their unique dual-power design to good effect by using the on-board diesel generator to provide power when working over non-electrified lines, electro-diesel No. E6030 heads through Kensington Olympia with 8M83, the 14.52 Hither Green – Willesden transfer freight on 30 June 1967.

The late Andrew Smith / authors collection

In the final months of steam operation most Saturday passenger workings on the South Western main line were, in the absence of the vital REP power units, powered by diesel locomotives. On 3 June 1967, Birmingham Railway Carriage & Wagon Co diesel-electric 1,550hp Type 3 No. D6543 heads through the sylvan setting of Clapham Cutting hauling a 12-car rake of TC units in their original drab overall blue livery. The headcode suggests that the service originated from Southampton Western Docks.

The late Andrew Smith / authors collection

A yard shunter looks on benignly as 'skinhead' Brush diesel-electric 1,250hp Type 2 No. D5518 passes Wimbledon with an Ilford Car Shed - Eastleigh empty stock transfer. This was during the period when the 1954 built AM7 Great Eastern Main Line Outer Suburban 4-car units were undergoing traction current conversion from 1,500v dc to 25kv ac in order to allow operation from the new voltage system. Following a serious collision in 1967 the opportunity was taken to rebuild No.D5518 as per the production batch specification, by having the troublesome Mirlees engine replaced, fitment of roof mounted headcode indicator boxes, blue star coupling code classification and uprated gearing to allow 90mph running.

Richard Simmons

Left - After steam had faded away on the Southern, local shunting and trip duties were entrusted to a wide variety of diesel classes, such as Drewry Car Co. 204hp 0-6-0 diesel-mechanical shunter No.D2286 seen in the sidings at Clapham Junction in October 1967, having wandered across South London from Hither Green. Local shunting, for which the 204hp diesels were intended, was already fast diminishing and facing a bleak future No.D2286 was withdrawn six months later. Breaking occurred at Fratton depot in June 1969. Young Master Jones, son of the photographer, dutifully records the 'cop' in his spotters' book. *Keith Jones*

Bottom - In the months following withdrawal of steam on the Southern Region, the authorities were often struggling to cover the workload. Intensive utilisation, together with a complete timetable recast, proved difficult to operate without practice and experience with the new traction. In October 1967 Birmingham Railway Carriage & Wagon Co. diesel-electric 1,550hp Type 3 No. D6536 was press-ganged into lending a hand at Clapham carriage sidings, in company with BR diesel-electric 350hp shunter No.D3221, drafted in from Feltham. *Keith Jones*

The Southern Region solution, when tasked with eliminating steam on the then non-electrified lines serving Oxted and East Sussex, was to develop their unique Diesel Electric Multiple Unit concept that used slow-revving English Electric engines as the power source, affectionately referred to as 'Thumpers'. In 1962 nineteen 3-car sets were constructed at Eastleigh with 8ft 6in wide bodies, necessary because of the restricted clearances in the tunnels between Tonbridge and Tunbridge Wells West. Shortly after introduction, DEMU No.1313 eases away from East Croydon with a Tunbridge Wells West – Victoria service. These units were capable of putting in creditable performances on the open country sections of this route, but the run up to town from here underlined the sluggish nature of the traction motors when operating at lower line speeds. Nevertheless these sturdy machines enjoyed lengthy careers; the last examples remaining in service until August 2004.

The On Line Video collection

The unmistakable sound of the 3D East Sussex Diesel Electric Multiple Unit's plying their trade amongst the incessant whine of Southern electrics was always a refreshing interlude. This summer 1978 view shows unit No.1310, in corporate rail blue livery with full yellow ends, approaching Clapham Junction with a Victoria - Uckfield service. The majority of the type were withdrawn following completion of the East Grinstead electrification scheme in 1987, although a few lingered on until 2004, so completing an impressive forty-two years service.

Pat Avery

As seen previously, after its brief sojourn on the Eastern Region during February 1961 assisting with electric train heating tests on coaching stock, BRCW 1,550hp diesel-electric Type 3 No. D6504 returned to familiar territory on the Southern and is seen heading a lengthy freight westwards through Woking. Renumbered as No. 33.004 in the TOPS reclassification of 1974, withdrawal did not occur until June 1991, more than 31 years after introduction to service. This locomotive was one of the few diesels to be broken up in-house at Eastleigh Works the following year.

Martin Upward

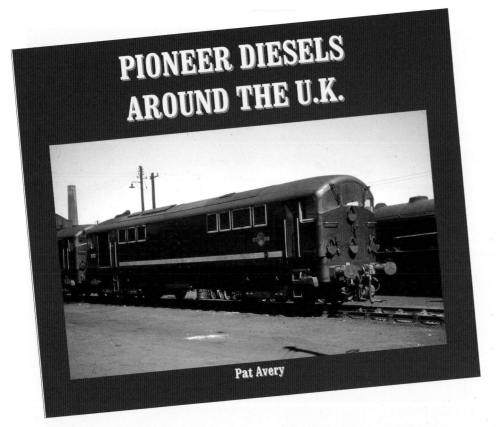